Body Systems: An Introduction

VISTA®
HIGHER LEARNING

Boston, Massachusetts

SCIENCE

We all have a body, but how much do you know about how yours works? Not much? Don't worry. We're here to take a look at six of the body's most important systems. You'll see what each one does and learn more about how they all work together. Are you ready to learn? Let's go!

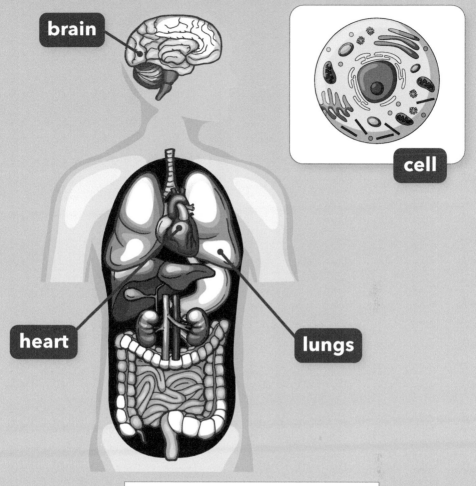

brain

cell

heart

lungs

37 trillion = 37,000,000,000,000

Before we look at body systems, let's first talk a bit about **cells**. Our bodies and all living things are made up of many small cells. In fact, there are about 37 trillion of them in every person's body. These cells are so small that you can't see them individually, but all life depends on them.

Cells come together to form different **tissues**. These body tissues make our **organs**. The brain, lungs, and heart are all important organs. They keep our bodies alive!

All those cells in the body need oxygen. Where does it come from, and how do the cells get it?

oxygen = O

Two systems do this work: the respiratory and circulatory systems. When we breathe, our lungs take in oxygen. This is the main job of the respiratory system. Next, the circulatory system takes over. Blood is pumped through the lungs by the heart. There, it picks up oxygen. Then, **blood vessels** carry that oxygen all around the body and deliver it to the cells. After that, they carry the blood back to the lungs to get more oxygen. Working together, these two systems provide the body with one of the most important items it needs for life. What a great team!

Respiratory System

Circulatory System

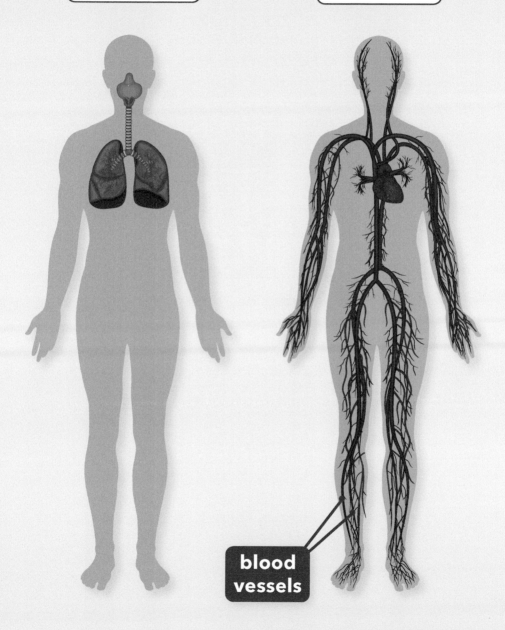

blood vessels

Body systems are very flexible and able to change according to the needs of the body. In other words, they **respond** to what we're doing. Here are a couple of examples.

This young woman is running, which takes more effort than usual. As a result, her cells need more oxygen than normal. She begins breathing faster, and her lungs start working harder. They fill with oxygen more quickly. Her heart beats faster, too, so the blood moves through the body more quickly. This gives her cells the extra oxygen they need.

Now let's think about a different situation. As you can see, this person isn't exercising, he's sleeping. Some people think that when you're sleeping, you *and* your body are not doing anything. That is most certainly not true!

Even when resting, our cells still need oxygen. They just need less of it because they aren't working that hard. As a result, when we sleep, we breathe more slowly, and our lungs fill with less air. Can you guess what happens to the heart when we sleep or rest? That's right! It beats more slowly.

Fun facts about the heart

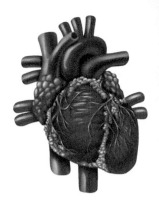

The heart is one of the most important organs in the body, and it's incredibly strong. It has to be! Here are some fun facts about the heart:

- The heart beats about 105,000 times a day, or about 70 to 80 times a minute for the average person.

- The heart is a muscle that's about the size of your closed hand.

- There are about 60,000 miles (95,000 kilometers) of blood vessels in the body. That means that the heart must pump blood all that distance, every day. It never has a break!

- Some people think the heart is on the left side of the body, but it's not. It's in the middle of your chest.

- Did you know the two halves of the heart have different jobs? The right-hand side of the heart pumps blood to the lungs. The left-hand side pumps blood and oxygen back into the body.

Fun facts about blood

Blood is a thick liquid that moves constantly through the body to bring **nutrients** and oxygen to cells. Here are some fun facts about blood:

- The average person has over one gallon of blood (five liters) in his or her body.

- All blood has red cells and white cells, which both have different jobs. Red blood cells carry oxygen to cells. White blood cells defend the body and keep us healthy by fighting anything bad that gets into our blood.

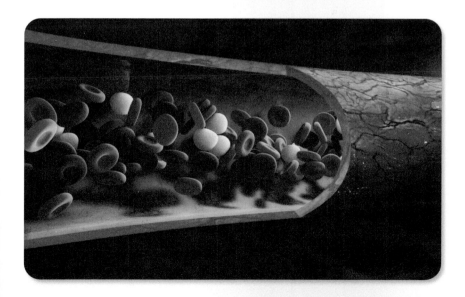

Not all our energy comes from the oxygen we breathe. This next system is very important, too!

The digestive system helps us get energy from the food we eat and the liquids we drink. Food goes into the stomach, where it's broken down by a strong acid. Then, those nutrients go into our blood to give the body energy and help it grow.

Digestive System

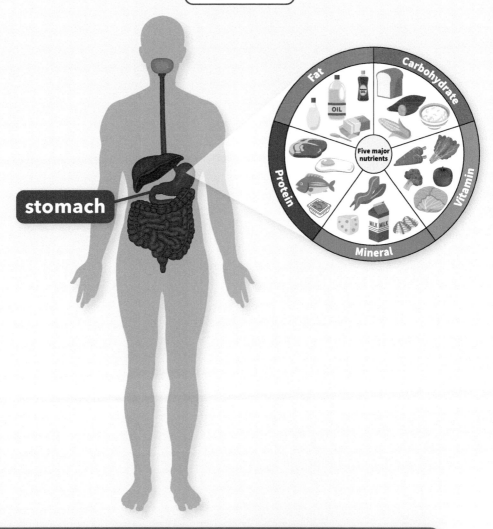

stomach

Five major nutrients

Fat · Carbohydrate · Vitamin · Mineral · Protein

KNOW IT ALL

The stomach is quite small. It's only about 12 inches (30.5 cm) long; however, it can hold about one quart (one liter) of food. Food normally stays in the stomach for three to five hours. Stomach **acid** not only helps break down food, but it also kills things in food that aren't good for us. It's a busy organ!

Look at this girl. She's having dinner, which means she should be giving her body the nutrients it needs. Because her food is healthy, it will give her body what it needs to grow and repair itself effectively. It will also give her energy for a long time, so she won't feel tired or hungry any time soon.

healthy food

unhealthy food

Not all food is the same, however. Some foods are unhealthy. They give us a lot of **calories** without many nutrients. They also often contain more sugar and fat than our bodies need.

When we eat unhealthy foods, our bodies often don't get the nutrients they need. This can cause us to feel hungry again quickly. These foods also give us energy for only a short time. We often feel tired and out of energy just a short while after eating them.

Now we know how the body gets the energy it needs, but what does it do with that energy? How does it use it?

One of the most common uses for body energy is movement. We need energy when we walk, run, jump, or do anything. The muscular system is what makes those actions possible.

Our **muscles** work in pairs to **contract** and relax. This allows them to do the work that results in movement. Blood carries oxygen and nutrients to the muscles, which break them down further and use them to move. Our muscles also use those nutrients to grow and develop.

Muscular System

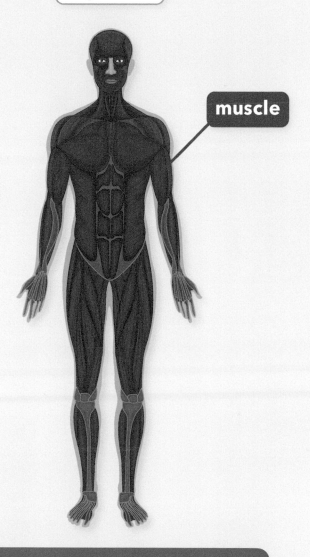

muscle

KNOW IT ALL

Did you know that there are over 650 muscles in the body? The heart is a muscle, but it isn't the strongest one. The strongest muscle is one that helps us chew when we eat.

Let's look at the muscular system in action. This young man is out shopping. But is he using his muscles? Yes, he's using lots of them!

The muscles in his hand are needed to hold the bags and stop them from falling on the ground. The muscles in his arm carry the bags and also move forward and backward to help him walk. The muscles in his legs contract and relax to make him walk. In addition, the muscles in his neck keep his head up so he can see where he's going. Everything we do uses muscles!

Nervous System

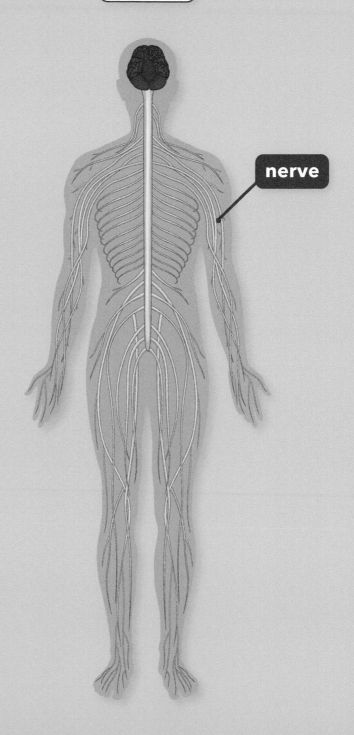

nerve

Let's move on to the nervous system. What does it do? It works with the brain. It sends, carries, and responds to messages.

The nervous system is how the body communicates all the important information it needs. There are billions of nerve cells in the human body, and the brain sends messages to most of them each day. These messages tell muscles and body parts to move in certain ways, work at certain speeds, and do things for different reasons.

Nerves throughout the body also send messages to the brain. They keep the body safe by saying things like, "That's hot!" "That hurts!" "That's dangerous!"

Look at what's happening in this situation. This woman was busy making dinner and wanted to check on her meal. However, that pot had been in the oven for a while, so it was very hot. She grabbed the cover to open it, and it **burned** her hand when she touched it. What happened next was all about her nervous system!

Her nerves recognized that she was experiencing pain and immediately sent a message to the brain. The brain recognized the danger of heat and responded by telling her to move her hand away quickly. Thanks to the nervous system, her **burn** isn't too bad!

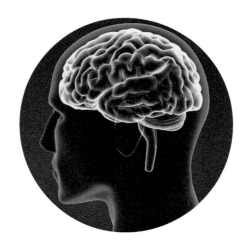

The Brain

Did you know that the human brain is large when compared to most other animals? It weighs about 3.3 pounds (1.5 kilos), which is about 2 percent of the weight of the average human body. Our large brains are working all the time, so they use about 20 percent of the oxygen and energy in our bodies.

The brain recognizes five senses: taste, smell, touch, hearing, and sight. Each sense is associated with an organ: the tongue, the nose, the skin, the ears, or the eyes. The way we understand the world around us depends on these senses and the messages they send to our brains. When you're awake, all the senses are sending millions of messages to the brain throughout the day. Your brain receives so many messages that it must learn to concentrate on the most important things you need.

Different parts of the brain do different things. For example, one part of the brain is concerned with hearing and language. Another part processes information from the eyes and senses. Yet another is responsible for movement, personality, speech, and thinking. Everything you hear, see, think, and do is controlled by the brain—even your dreams and your memories!

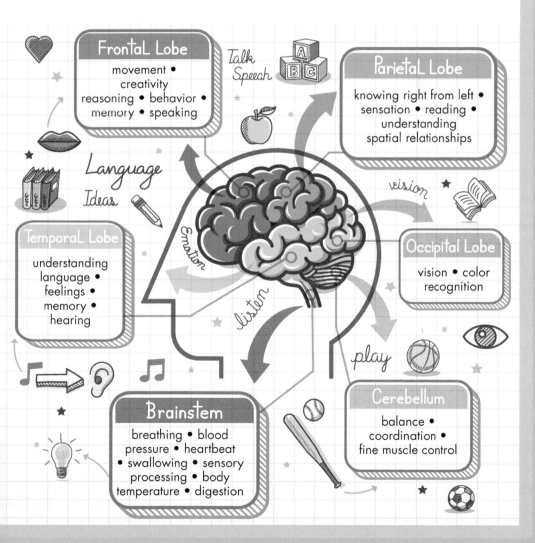

Frontal Lobe
movement •
creativity
reasoning • behavior •
memory • speaking

Talk
Speech

Parietal Lobe
knowing right from left •
sensation • reading •
understanding
spatial relationships

Language
Ideas

vision

Temporal Lobe
understanding
language •
feelings •
memory •
hearing

Emotion

Occipital Lobe
vision • color
recognition

listen

play

Brainstem
breathing • blood
pressure • heartbeat
• swallowing • sensory
processing • body
temperature • digestion

Cerebellum
balance •
coordination •
fine muscle control

Skeletal System

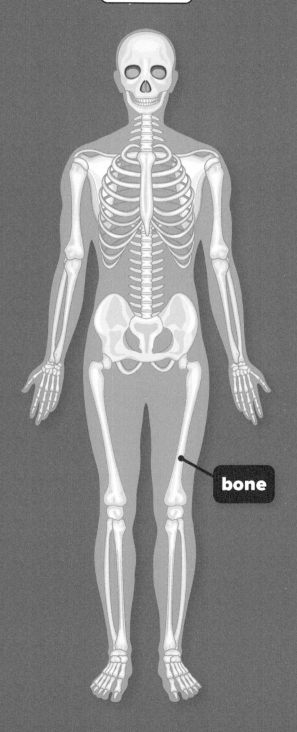

bone

It's time to move on to the final system we'll be looking at today: the skeletal system. The **skeleton** is the name we give to all our bones together. It works as a frame to support the body. It works together with the muscular system to help us move so we can stand, sit, walk, and run.

Without bones, our bodies would look very funny!

skull

Remember! When doing sports or riding bikes, a helmet is the best way to protect *your* very important brain!

What else does the skeletal system do? One very important job of this system is to keep our organs safe. Organs are soft and delicate, so they are easily damaged. Bones are hard and can keep them from harm. The skull, which is the main bone in the head, is there to **protect** the brain. The ribs are the bones that come from the back and go around the chest. One of their main jobs is to protect the heart and lungs.

The young man on the left has just hit his head. He could have really done some damage to his brain. However, his strong skull was there to protect him and keep his brain safe—good for him!

EXTRA! HANDS ARE INCREDIBLE!

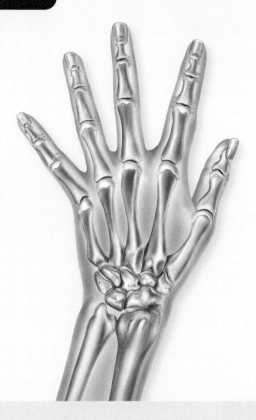

There are 27 bones in your hand. These bones make our hands flexible and able to move in several different ways. We use more than 30 muscles to move our thumb and fingers alone! There are also over 25 **joints** in each hand. This allows us to move our hands and fingers in several important and different ways.

According to scientists, one of the biggest differences between humans and most animals is that we have thumbs that are different from our fingers. Because of that, we can hold and carry things better with our hands. Try writing, eating, or holding a cup without using your thumb. It's difficult!

And there you have it: an introduction to the human body and just a few of its important systems. The respiratory system brings in oxygen. The circulatory system carries it around the body through the blood. The digestive system breaks down our food to give us energy and help us repair our bodies and grow. The muscular and skeletal systems work together to help us move. The nervous system keeps the body safe.

cell smallest basic part of an animal or plant

tissue a group of basic body parts that form a larger part of the body

organ a part of the body that has a special job

blood vessel a long thin part of the body that carries blood to or from the heart

respond to act in a certain way as the result of another action or thing that happened; to react

nutrients items usually found in food in food that the body needs to be healthy and stay alive

acid a strong chemical liquid that can change things like food into smaller parts

calorie a unit of energy, usually used to measure how much energy there is in food

muscle a part of the body that relaxes or tightens in order to move or do things

contract to grow shorter and tighten

nerve a part of the body that reacts to pain and other things and sends messages to the brain

burn (*v.*) to hurt something with fire or heat, (*n.*) a place hurt or harmed by heat or fire

skeleton the framework of bones inside the body that holds it up and carries its weight

protect to keep something safe from danger

joint the point where two or more bones meet and are able to move